+ JMJ +

dear baby Braunlin ♥

oh, we are _so_
excited that you
are on your way!

your cousins enjoyed this book
for many years, and we all
hope that you do, too!

God bless you!

we love you ♥

Great Aunt Mollie & Great Uncle Jimmy
and your cousins —
Pete, Amelia & Elijah,
Isaac, Gabe, Gemma,
Anne, & Simon

the Maimones

W9-CDL-108

JESUS AND MARY

Contents

These books, originally published under four separate covers, were first issued in 1953. This combined edition is published by

© THE NEUMANN PRESS

2001

JESUS & MARY   ISBN 1-930873-42-5

www.neumannpress.com

PRINTED AND PUBLISHED IN THE UNITED STATES OF AMERICA
THE NEUMANN PRESS, LONG PRAIRIE, MINNESOTA

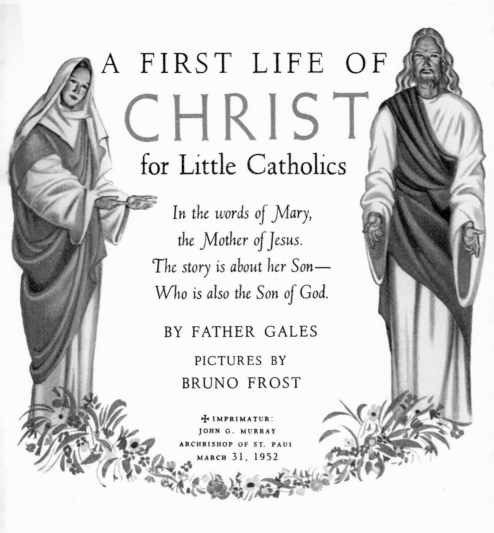

A FIRST LIFE OF
CHRIST
for Little Catholics

*In the words of Mary,
the Mother of Jesus.
The story is about her Son—
Who is also the Son of God.*

BY FATHER GALES

PICTURES BY
BRUNO FROST

✠ IMPRIMATUR:
JOHN G. MURRAY
ARCHBISHOP OF ST. PAUL
MARCH 31, 1952

The Neumann Press
LONG PRAIRIE, MINNESOTA

When I was a girl in Galilee I loved to think about the promise God made to send a Saviour. Every Jewish girl longed to be His mother. One day an angel came to me and said, "God wants to send His Son into the world. His name shall be called Jesus. Will you be His mother?"

With all my heart I said yes. God had chosen a good man named Joseph to be my husband. He would help me care for the Baby Jesus.

Just before Jesus was born, Joseph had to journey up to Bethlehem, the home of his father's people, to register. Kind Joseph had a donkey for me to ride. But it was a long journey. I was tired when we arrived. And there was no room in the inn.

After a search, Joseph found space in a stable where we could rest.

There Jesus was born. I wrapped Him in swaddling clothes and laid Him in the manger.

Soon some shepherds came, and fell on their knees
before the Babe. Angels had come to them in the
field near by to tell them that a Saviour had been
born in Bethlehem who was Christ the Lord.

Kings came too, from the far lands of the East, and they brought rich gifts for the Baby in the manger. They had seen His star shining in the sky, and they had come to adore the greatest King of all.

But there was one king who did not rejoice. This was wicked Herod who ruled in Jerusalem. He planned to have Jesus killed. But God sent an angel to warn Joseph in a dream, and to tell him to take us to Egypt.

When Herod was dead, an angel told Joseph that we could return safely to Nazareth. How glad we were to be among our friends and relatives again!

The years passed in quiet happiness for us. Jesus grew up to be a strong Boy. He was a joy to everyone, even though they did not know He was God.

When Jesus was twelve years old, we took Him
to the temple in Jerusalem. He felt at home there
because it was the house of God, His Father.

Jesus was not with our company when we started back toward Nazareth. So Joseph and I turned back to find Him. We found Him in the temple, talking with the teachers. They marveled to find a Boy so wise.

The happy years of childhood passed. Jesus became a grown Man. It was time for Him to be about His work of showing men how to live to please their heavenly Father.

Jesus went from place to place, telling people about loving and serving God.

He picked out twelve men and trained them to be apostles. He also gave them power to do God's work. The apostles left homes and families to follow Jesus.

Jesus cured the sick and the lame. He made the blind see again. He also brought a boy and a girl back from the dead. Jesus wanted to show the people that He was God by doing what only God can do.

Jesus loved to have little children about Him.
When the apostles tried to keep them from Him,
for fear they would be in His way, Jesus said,
"Let the little children come to Me, for of such
is the kingdom of heaven."

Jesus told His followers that they must believe
in God's goodness and power. They were not to
worry about anything in this world. "See how
God takes care of the birds," Jesus said.

"Your Father in heaven feeds them. He loves you much more than the birds. He will take even better care of you!" And Jesus taught them to pray, saying, "Our Father, Who art in heaven—"

Jesus taught many lessons by telling beautiful stories; these were so simple that everyone could understand them. Some stories were about shepherds, because so many of the people were shepherds.

Jesus talked about a happy shepherd who
found a lamb which had been lost. He told about
a father rejoicing when his wandering son came
back home. That is how God feels when one of
His disobedient children is truly sorry and promises
to be good again.

One day five thousand people followed Jesus into the country, to hear Him teach. When mealtime came, no one wanted to leave. But there was no village near where they could buy food. Jesus felt sorry for the people.

A boy had a basket of loaves and fishes. Jesus called the boy and blessed this bit of food. It fed the five thousand with some to spare! Then Jesus said: "Some day I will give you My Body as food for your souls."

The men who ruled in our country heard how
the people loved Jesus. They began to hate Him.
They thought that Jesus would try to take over
the government and have Himself crowned King.
They forgot that Jesus said, "My kingdom is
not of this world."

Jesus knew that His time on earth was grow-
ing short. He told the apostles to meet Him in an
upper room for His Last Supper. There He gave
to His apostles the most wonderful gift of all—

His own Body and Blood in the form of bread and wine. He gave His apostles and their followers the power to do the same in remembrance of Him.

So when you receive Holy Communion, you receive Jesus Himself, just as the apostles did that night at the first Mass.

Then Jesus went into a garden to pray. He was willing to suffer for the sins of all men. Judas, one of His apostles, brought to the garden the men who wanted to kill Him.

Pontius Pilate condemned Jesus to death. It was a bitter sorrow to watch my beloved Son dying on the cross! But even in His suffering, Jesus prayed for His enemies: "Father, forgive them, for they know not what they are doing."

Hanging on the cross, He asked His beloved apostle John to look after me. He asked God in heaven to forgive the people who caused His suffering. And He thought of you. As He died He gave Himself to His Father in heaven.

Jesus was buried in a tomb, but I knew that
this was not the end of His wonderful life. On
Easter Sunday, when I came to the tomb, it was
empty. The great stone was rolled away from the
door. Jesus appeared to me, risen from the grave.
Now even doubters would know that He was
God indeed!

Jesus appeared to His apostles, too, to tell them that they must go through all the world teaching the Word of God to all men.

Forty days later He blessed us and went up to heaven. But He did not forget us. Ten days later He sent the Holy Spirit to stay with the Church until the end of the world.

And when the end of my earthly life came, Jesus took my soul and body up to heaven to be with Him forever and ever.

I am always ready to listen when you talk to me, for I am your heavenly Mother. I will be glad to talk to Jesus about your needs, if you ask me to do this. And He will always do anything that will help you to come to Us in heaven.

Three Miracles of Jesus

by *ELIZABETH PHELAN*

pictures by *STEELE SAVAGE*

NIHIL OBSTAT: John A. Goodwine, J.C.D., *Censor Librorum*
IMPRIMATUR: ✠ Francis Cardinal Spellman, *Archbishop of New York*
October 10, 1961

CANA

One day Jesus and some friends climbed the green hills of Galilee to Cana. They were going to a wedding feast there.

It was a fine spring day. The air was warm, and the sun was shining. Jesus and His friends talked together as they climbed.

Soon they reached the bride's home. Mary, the Mother of Jesus, was already there. In a little while, they were enjoying the feast together.

But after a time, Mary saw that the supply of wine was getting low. She thought, "The bride and bridegroom will feel bad if there is no wine left for some of the guests."

Then Mary turned to the servants and said, "Do whatever Jesus asks you to do."

Jesus told the servants to fill some empty jars with water, and take them to the chief steward, who was in charge of the feast.

When the steward tasted from one of the jars, he was very surprised. He said to the bridegroom, "This isn't water! This is wine, and it is much better than the wine we have been drinking up to now. Why did you save

the best wine until the end of the feast?"

Everyone stared. They knew that Jesus of
Nazareth had performed a miracle. He had
changed water into wine.

This was the first miracle of Jesus. Three
years would pass before He would perform
an even greater one. On Holy Thursday, He
would change wine into His own blood.

JESUS WALKS ON THE WATER

One evening, the apostles were rowing across the sea when a strong wind began to blow. Soon the sea was covered with white-caps and the little boat rocked from side to side. As the wind blew harder and harder, the waves slapped against the boat.

Suddenly the apostles saw a shadowy
figure on the water.

"Who is that?" one of them whispered.

"It is the Lord," cried Peter. "Lord, let
me walk on the water, too!"

Jesus held out His hand, and Peter
stepped out of the swaying boat. He took a
few steps across the rough water. Then Peter
looked down at the sea, and thought with
fear, "I have nothing to hold onto. If I step
into the water, I shall surely drown!" At
that moment, he began to sink into the sea.

"Lord, help me!" Peter shouted in a voice that could be heard above the noise of the wind and waves.

Jesus walked over to Peter and helped him back into the boat.

Peter sat down, shivering with the cold. He was ashamed, because his faith in Jesus had been weak.

"Peter," said Jesus in a sad voice, "why do you have so little faith? If you had only believed in Me, you would have been able to walk on the water."

Jesus meant that He wants all people to trust in Him. Once before, He had said, "Anything is possible for him who believes in Me." Jesus wants us to have faith in Him. Then if we pray to Him, He will help us with whatever we are doing.

LOAVES AND FISHES

It was beginning to get dark, and the huge crowd of people who had listened to Jesus preach all day were tired and hungry.

Jesus said to Philip, "Buy some food so that we may feed these people."

"Where will we get enough money to feed five thousand people?" Philip asked.

"Surely some one here has food," Jesus replied calmly.

Andrew said, "Here is a small boy who has something to eat. But he has only five loaves of bread and two fishes."

The boy held out his food to Jesus. Jesus smiled at him and took the loaves and fishes. He blessed the food and said to His apostles, "Give this to the crowd."

The apostles looked at each other, for they could not believe their ears. How could so little food feed five thousand people?

But Jesus was waiting for the apostles to do as He asked. Slowly, they began to walk through the crowd, dividing the food among them.

The people sat on the green hillside. The grass smelled sweet and the cool breeze felt very good to them. Never had food tasted more delicious than the bread and fishes the apostles were handing to them.

At last they finished eating, and Jesus said to His apostles, "Gather up the leftover food." When they had done this, the remaining food filled twelve baskets!

The miracle of the loaves and fishes was wonderful. But the apostles would soon see something even more wonderful. At the Last Supper, Jesus would take bread and change it into His own body.

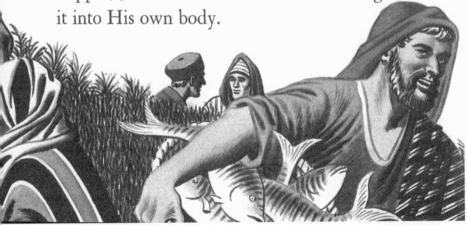

We cannot see Jesus multiply loaves and
fishes, for that happened a long time ago.
But we can see bread changed into His body.
Every day, at Mass, the priest changes bread
into the body of Jesus.

HAIL MARY
FOR LITTLE CATHOLICS

BY SISTER MARY ST. PAUL OF MARYKNOLL

PICTURES BY STEFFIE LERCH

Nihil obstat: JOHN A. GOODWINE J.C.D., Censor Librorum
Imprimatur: ✠ FRANCIS CARDINAL SPELLMAN, Archbishop of New York
April 2, 1957

IN THE little town
of Nazareth, far
across the sea, lived
a lovely girl named
Mary.

MARY was the most
beautiful girl that God
ever made.

God said, "There will
never be another girl
as holy and beautiful
as Mary is."

God loved Mary very
much. And that is why
she was so holy and
beautiful. God put His
own goodness and
beauty into Mary.

MARY loved everything
that God made.
She loved the big blue sky.
She loved the big white clouds.
She loved the birds,
the flowers
and all the little animals
that God made.
Mary loved all the people, too,
because God had made them.
And above all, Mary loved
to do everything that God said.

Now you know everybody wasn't good
all the time, as Mary was.

In fact, people had been so bad
that God had to shut the doors of heaven.

No one could go to heaven to see God.

This made Mary very sad.

MARY knew the doors
of heaven were shut.
   She used to say
in her prayers,
   "Hurry up dear God,
and send your Son
to save us.
   "Please make someone
good enough to be
His mother."

ONE day God said
to His angel named Gabriel,
  "Gabriel, do you see
that little town of Nazareth
on earth?
Go there and find
My loveliest daughter.
Her name is Mary.
She is going to marry
Joseph, the carpenter.
Ask Mary to be
the mother of My Son."

Mary was busy when Angel Gabriel
came. She was surprised to see him.

Angel Gabriel bowed before her.

He said, "Hail Mary, full of grace!
The Lord is with thee."

Then he told her that God wanted her
to be the mother of Jesus.

MARY was surprised to know
that God had picked her out
to be the mother of Jesus.
She was very happy.

"Of course," said Mary.
"I will do whatever God wants."

AFTER Angel Gabriel had left,
Mary went to see her cousin Elizabeth.
She got on her donkey
and rode over the hills.

She was so happy that she sang
along the way.

"See how happy Mary is,"
said the people.

WHEN Mary came, Elizabeth said,
"Blessed art thou among women,
and blessed is the fruit of thy womb,
Jesus."

God had let Elizabeth know
that Mary would be the mother of Jesus.

After a while
Jesus was born.
   Saint Joseph
was there to protect
Jesus and Mary.
   Jesus grew up
to be great.
He opened the doors
of heaven.
Now all the people
of the world
might go in.
   Jesus was
the Son of God!

THIS is how Jesus opened the doors of heaven.
He let some bad men nail Him to a big cross.

God said, "The big cross that holds Jesus
will be the key to open the doors of heaven."

Jesus on the cross is the key
that opens heaven for you, for me,
for everybody!

And when Jesus died, He gave Mary to us
for our mother.

Holy Mary, Mother of God, pray for us sinners, now and at the hour of our death.

Amen.

Hail Mary, full of grace!
The Lord is with thee.
Blessed art thou among women,
and blessed is the fruit
of thy womb, Jesus.
Holy Mary, Mother of God,
pray for us sinners,
now and at the hour
of our death.
Amen.

Our Lady of Fatima

by EVE ROUKE

Pictures by
WILLIAM DE J. RUTHERFOORD

NIHIL OBSTAT: John A. Goodwine, J.C.D., *Censor Librorum*
IMPRIMATUR: ✠ Francis Cardinal Spellman, *Archbishop of New York*
December 7, 1960

One day, at a moment chosen by God, a wonderful thing happened near the village of Fatima in a country called Portugal. The story begins with three little shepherd children.

Lucia dos Santos was ten years old. Her cousins
Jacinta and Francisco Marto were younger. On
this day, the three children took their sheep to
a pasture called the Cova da Iria.

In the pasture, Lucia, Jacinta, and Francisco began to build make-believe castles with rocks and stones. Suddenly, they saw a bright flash.

The children thought the flash was lightning, so they decided to get their sheep and run home before it rained. But all of a sudden they saw a Beautiful Lady standing on a little tree.

The Lady was really standing on that tree. She looked so different from their friends that the children were afraid. They started to run away.

The Beautiful Lady told them not to be afraid. She said she was from heaven and that she wanted to see them the next month, to tell them of our Lord's wishes. Then she floated up into the sky.

Such a thing had never happened in Fatima, and most of the people in the village did not believe the story of the Beautiful Lady.

This made the children sad. But no matter what the people said, Lucia, Jacinta, and Francisco knew the Lady would come again. So the next month they went back to the Cova. And there they saw her again.

Some people still did not believe that the Lady was real. The wicked mayor of Fatima was so angry that he put the children in jail. He tried to make them say that their story was not true.

Even the village priest did not believe that the children had really seen the Lady. But he could not make them change their story.

The next month the Lady came again. And the next month. And the next month. And the month after that. Many people from the village followed the children to the Cova. They could not see the Lady, but they knew she was there.

The Lady told the children that people should pray the rosary every day, and do penance, and make sacrifices for sinners. She said our Lord was sad because so many people committed sins.

By this time thousands of people believed the children's story and went with them to the Cova. When the Beautiful Lady came for the sixth time, a great miracle took place.

The sun danced and trembled and spun like a pinwheel. It zigzagged toward the earth. Then it became so pale that everyone could look straight at it without blinking. This was the sign from God that our Lady had promised.

Not long after this, Jacinta and Francisco died. They were so happy to know they would go to heaven where they could be with the Beautiful Lady forever!

But Lucia knew, because our Lady had told her
so, that she was to live and tell others what she
and her cousins had seen at the Cova. In time,
Lucia became a nun and did God's will by living
for Him, and praying, and making sacrifices.

The Blessed Mother visited Fatima in 1917.
Now a very big church is there. Many people go
to Fatima to pray. Many who are sick go to be
cured, and sometimes they are made well.

But most people who go to Fatima learn that our Lord wants them always to remember Him, and to pray and make sacrifices. That is the real reason the Beautiful Lady came to Fatima.

The
Neumann
Press